Everyday Virtues

John W. Crossin, O.S.F.S.

Paulist Press
New York/Mahwah, New Jersey

Library of Congress Cataloging-in-Publication Data

Crossin, John W.
Everyday virtues / John W. Crossin.
    p.   cm.—(IlluminationBooks)
   Includes bibliographical references (p.   ).
   ISBN: 0-8091-4087-X
   1. Virtues. 2. Christian ethics—Catholic authors. I. Title.
II. Series.
BV4630 .C75 2002
241′.4—dc21

                                      2002006281

Published by Paulist Press
997 Macarthur Boulevard
Mahwah, New Jersey 07430

www.paulistpress.com

Printed and bound in the
United States of America

Contents

Acknowledgment

I wish to thank Carole Greene and David Gibson of the Catholic News Service for their graciousness in encouraging me to publish this book. These essays originally appeared in the *Faith Alive* series and are published with the permission of the Catholic News Service. They have been revised for publication in the IlluminationBooks series.

IlluminationBooks
A Foreword

When this series was launched in 1994, I wrote that Illumination-Books were conceived to "bring to light wonderful ideas, helpful information, and sound spirituality in concise, illustrative, readable, and eminently practical works on topics of current concern."

In keeping with this premise, among the first books were offerings by well-known authors Joyce Rupp *(Little Pieces of Light...Darkness and Personal Growth)* and Basil Pennington *(Lessons from the Monastery That Touch Your Life)*. In addition, there were titles by up-and-coming authors and experts in the fields of spirituality and psychology.

These books covered a wide array of topics: joy, controlling stress and anxiety, personal growth, discernment, caring for others, the mystery of the Trinity, celebrating the woman you are, and facing your own desert experiences.

The continued goal of the series is to provide great ideas, helpful steps, and needed inspiration in small volumes. Each of the books offers a new opportunity for the reader to explore possibilities and embrace practicalities that can be employed in everyday life. Thus, among the new and noteworthy themes for readers to discover are these: how to be more receptive to the love in our lives, simple ways to structure a personal day of recollection, a creative approach to enjoy reading sacred scriptures, and spiritual and psychological methods of facing discouragement.

Like the IlluminationBooks before them, forthcoming volumes are meant to be a source of support—without requiring an inordinate amount of time or prior preparation. To this end, each small work stands on its own. The hope is that the information provided not only will be nourishing in itself but also will encourage further exploration in the area.

When we view the world through spiritual eyes, we appreciate that sound knowledge is really useful only when it can set the stage for *metanoia*, the conversion of our hearts. Each of the IlluminationBooks is designed to contribute in some small but significant way to this process. So, it is with a sense of hope and warm wishes that I offer this particular title and the rest of the series to you.

–*Robert J. Wicks*
General Editor, IlluminationBooks

Introduction

Taking the opportunities each day to practice virtues such as patience, humor or understanding slowly builds an inner orientation to God that leads to holiness. *With this practice comes a certain* inner peace. *This is the tranquility of the life well lived, the confidence in choices well made, the inner harmony of grace and nature.*

In the four chapters which follow, we will meditate on some of the virtues for daily living. These chapters will concern themselves with:

(1) the foundations for virtuous living;
(2) the theological virtues of faith, hope and love;
(3) the moral virtues lived each day; and
(4) the daily cultivation of virtues.

Certain basic themes will run through this entire book. One key theme is *the importance of human relationships*. We often learn how to live through the example of others. I believe that we learn virtues in relationships. Our friends, family and colleagues help to make us who we are. We are not isolated individuals but persons who are always interacting with others. Our choices are very much affected by the quality of our relationships. There is much truth in the adage: "Tell me who your friends are, and I'll tell you who you are."

Personal experiences are stressed throughout this work. In these chapters, I share some of my own life experiences and those of people I know. I hope that you will find these examples helpful in reflecting on your own experience.

The everyday virtues are concrete and related to our experiences of daily living. The key idea here is to *work with the present possibilities*. Every day offers opportunities to be gentle, kind and supportive. It is in the present moment that the spiritual life is lived.

In stressing the present moment, I am reflecting my own commitment to the Salesian spiritual tradition. I am a follower of St. Francis de Sales and St. Jane de Chantal. Their focus was on living the virtues each day in imitation of Christ. These chapters are my own reflection on their spiritual heritage. There is a profound Christian theology underlying the Salesian tradition of virtue, though it will not be our major concern in this small volume.[1]

In the Catholic tradition, virtues unite our deepest longings and our best knowledge. They bring together our thoughts and feelings, our intuitions and scientific knowledge. The virtues integrate our total humanity. They strengthen us. By definition, *virtue implies strength.*

There are many virtues. *These virtues are linked.* They flow into and out of one another. Many times our descriptions of them will overlap. Ultimately each virtue can be seen as a dimension or aspect of love.

Love is the root of all the other virtues. Love is what we humans long for throughout our lives. Most profoundly, the fullness of love is the gift of the Holy Spirit. The third person of the Trinity is that inner love which transforms our hearts and gives our virtues a spiritual depth beyond our complete comprehension or imagination. It is the Spirit of Love that enables us *to live like Christ, to become holy.* This requires daily conscientious decisions to love as Christ loved. Everyday virtues are practical. In the chapters that follow, we will see some striking examples of this practice.

Chapter One

The Foundations for Virtuous Living: Relationships, Example and Virtues

G od often speaks to us—wordlessly—through the example of others. Silent example speaks eloquently. It speaks to the deeper, more important realities that can be missed in the rush of daily living. Example can speak to us most profoundly of love for God. My experience in Romania in the early nineties brought this home to me in a striking way.

Meditation on the virtues of a hidden martyr

I met some wonderful people on my eight-day trip to Romania. I met a living martyr there and I still don't know his name. Our meeting happened by accident—as many very important things do. God's providence is surprising and inscrutable.

It was the next to last day of our trip. The priest who served as chancellor for the diocese was driving us to an airport for the trip back to Bucharest. We made good time traveling to the neighboring town, so we made an eventful stop to leave some paperwork with an older priest. The chancellor told us that the priest had been in prison for seventeen years. I had to wonder what the prison was like. On our first night in Bucharest, by misadventure, we had wound up staying in a local hotel. The rooms were clean and neat. The hard bed, however, reminded me of my days camping out in the Boy Scouts. Luckily, I liked camping out! I wondered if there were beds in prison.

When we reached the elderly priest's church, it was near the center of town—a space no larger than a high school classroom. He was right in the middle of preparing a couple for their wedding. I still remember, for some reason, that they were all sitting on hard-backed chairs. There were several icons on the walls. The chancellor told us that the place overflowed with people on Sundays.

The priest, surprised at our visit, rose and greeted the chancellor warmly. He wore a black cassock and had a white beard. He seemed to be in his midseventies. He definitely fit my vision of what an Eastern rite Catholic priest should look like.

Sister Lucianne, my colleague and guide, and I were introduced to him. We carried on a brief conversation with him, with the chancellor serving as interpreter. The priest struck me as feisty. He spoke of the challenge of educating

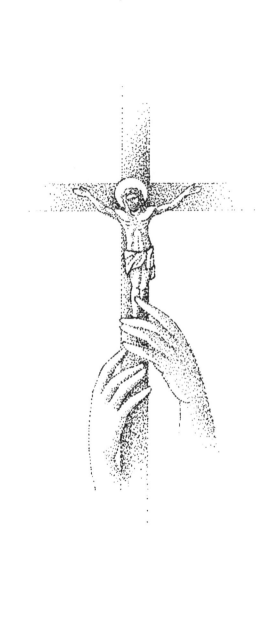

his people in the faith. He obviously relished the opportunities afforded by the country's newfound freedom. We parted cordially.

In the airplane, sister asked me if I had seen the look in his eyes. I said no, I hadn't noticed. She explained that she had seen that same look in the eyes of other long-term prisoners—priests, sisters and laity—whom she had met on her previous visits to Romania. She called it a "mystical look." People in prison had to go deep within themselves in order to survive. These survivors had deep spiritual roots—and many scars as well.

On our second night in Bucharest we had stayed in the newly-refurbished papal embassy. For over forty years it had been in communist hands. More precisely, it had been used by the secret police. It was an eerie experience, celebrating Mass the next morning in a place where people had been tortured, and perhaps had died. I wondered if this priest had been tortured too.

Suffering is a disconcerting part of our lives and our faith. We shy away from suffering but it touches every life in some way. The profound suffering of Jesus on the cross is a constant reminder of the reality of human suffering. Our tradition presents us with the *King of Love*—on the cross.

Martyrs are people of character with incredibly deep commitment. Even after all those years in prison, this priest was still doing his work—educating people in the faith, preparing a couple for marriage, and so on. He clearly knew what he believed. And he obviously was still putting his faith into practice. Martyrs are followers of Christ. The priest's church, his garb, his eyes spoke of

Christ. This living martyr was the icon. In some mysterious way, in encountering him I encountered Christ.

I don't even know the man's name, yet this is not important. Like the artists who built the great medieval cathedrals, his anonymity sends me directly to Jesus. If I had gotten to know him, I probably would have found that he had strengths and weaknesses like us all. Today's hidden martyrs, like martyrs of old, arc human just like us. Their lives speak of commitment, not perfection. Their example is very challenging. They are our contemporaries—but they cannot be dismissed as irrelevant. They know that our choices and actions are important—urging us to continue to work hard rather than think our actions are insignificant.

The example of such martyrs reminds us that Christ is never far away—he is near at hand. Nor are acts of heroism far from us. People we encounter in our daily lives model Christ's love for us—though not usually in such striking ways as this priest did for me. Most example is more ordinary, but no less profound.

The influence of the past: People make a difference

What people have influenced our lives? Our parents to be sure. I am still discovering ways that I resemble my parents. I like to be "always busy" like my mother; I enjoy sports like my father. I love the Mass like both my parents. Our parents and other relatives—a special aunt or uncle for example—may be a continuing influence in our lives.

Other people's influence on us may be a little less obvious than that of our parents and relatives. A special teacher, friend or coach might have pointed us in the right direction for our future life and work. Even a small gesture, such as the encouragement by a friend to go on a retreat, may be all that is necessary to set us on a new course.

The more we think about it, the further back in history we can go in detecting the influences on our lives. The bishops at the Council of Baltimore in the last century had a profound influence on me, even though I never met them. They gave the impetus to the writing of the catechism that is still called the "Baltimore Catechism."

I will always know the answer to the question: *Why did God make you?* The catechism answers that I learned at St. Matthew's parish school in Philadelphia have stayed with me both consciously and unconsciously. I learned that I am on earth to know, love and serve God. My two decades of studying and teaching Catholic theology have amplified but not modified this answer. The writers of that catechism had a profound influence on many in my generation of young (now middleaged) Catholics.

A more subtle influence from the past comes through the shape of the buildings in which we worship. The magnificent Gothic cathedrals, with their high ceilings, pull us up to heaven and remind us of the transcendence of God—that God is truly above us. The contemporary churches-in-the-round make us look at one another and encourage us to pray together. They are the churches of the "people of God," emphasized at the Second Vatican Council (1961–65). They remind us that God truly is with us in our community.

The play of light penetrating the stained-glass windows of these churches is fascinating to see. The images of apostles and saints connect us with our spiritual history. They remind us of our forebears who passed faith on to us. Some of these men and women were so illustrious as to be canonized saints; others were of the no less important "All Saints Day" variety.

We marvel at the faith that led to such magnificent dedication and creativity. Such creativity is evident in the great thinkers in our tradition. They synthesized theology with the questions of their time so well that they continue to influence us today. St. Augustine of Hippo (d. 430) is one such outstanding person.

Augustine could be a man living in our time, rather than in the last days of the Roman Empire. His faults are ours. He is well known for his early lapse from the Christian faith into which he had been baptized. Brilliant and ambitious, he lived with his common-law wife and sired an illegitimate son. His *Confessions* tell of his soul's long and difficult journey to God. His early life could be a modern romantic novel. His mother, Monica, like many contemporary parents, attained her sanctity in praying relentlessly for him during the time of his great ambitions. After his conversion, Augustine became one of the most brilliant of the early theologians. His thought, whether on the Just War or the relationship of the City of God to the earthly city, influences how we think today. His reflections on the virtue of love still offer profound insights for us.

Another of our saintly predecessors, Jane de Chantal (d. 1641), offers a different type of rootedness in our past. She was a wife, mother, widow, foundress, innovator and mystic. With Francis de Sales, she founded the order of the Visitation sisters. The sisters were, in the original intention, not only to visit the sick but also to accept the physically handicapped as members. Neither of these things was done by sisters in the seventeenth century, but she initiated the changes we now take for granted.

Our lives are part of a rich flow of church history that shapes our present. Whether through saints, artists, friends, relatives or parents, the past becomes our present through others. A great spiritual and cultural heritage comes to us through them.

Virtues in families

The most intimate place for living the spiritual life is the family. As I noted above, I am still discovering what I learned from my parents—and from my two brothers, my sister, and my aunts and uncles. A key virtue in all of our family learning is humor. What is the latest foolish, inattentive or just-plain-crazy thing that you have done? (Be honest now!) Sharing a joke on ourselves, acknowledging the stupid things we all do and learning to laugh at ourselves is central to developing the other virtues we need in families and in all our relationships.

Humor, an aspect of humility, helps us to keep life in perspective. In fact, we can even come to treasure those comical moments when the joke is on us. Such moments teach us not to expect perfection—from ourselves or from others. "The perfect is the enemy of the good" is a bit of wisdom we might ponder.

At times our expectations of ourselves and of others might be a little unrealistic. We expect only the best.

Our team must win every soccer game. Our children's grades must be all A's. Our house must always be in order. We must be caught up with our work. Yet, in fact, we are far from perfect. So it's best to keep life in perspective.

With humor comes the insight that we are not in complete control of our life. We work legitimately to achieve worthwhile goals such as financial support for our family members. Yet, many things happen to us that we do not expect. Ultimately, God is in control.

Just like an infant learning to walk, we have to learn to let go. For adults, this letting go is a daily thing. It is also a deeply spiritual reality. God calls us to let go of our expectations and our accustomed ways of doing things, for our own good and the good of others. This "letting go" calls for more than a little patience. The virtue of patience is immediately applicable every day. We need patience while we wait in line in stores, in town or at the mall. We need patience in traffic in our congested urban areas as we drive to work, or to the mall to wait in line!

At home we need patience with the unending questions of little children, the teenagers' distancing and quest for identity, the concerns of our neighbors and the intrusion of unexpected events. We also need patience with ourselves. Change of our own way of doing things, or of our expectations, is slow. Growth takes time. As we become older, we see how change is possible, but difficult. Overcoming our own doubts and insecurities can be slow. We seem to fall into the same habits of impatience, uncivility and uncharitableness again and again. Thus we realize our need for God's help—our need to pray.

I have been privileged to be with several families when they pray. Sometimes this prayer takes the form of an extended "grace" before the evening meal. One couple I know prays in the living room with their children before they go to bed. Each member of the family takes a turn in doing a Bible reading, reading about the life of a saint or lighting a candle. Each one has an opportunity to offer a petition for others—family members, friends, schoolmates or colleagues at work. Such an experience reminds both children and adults of the importance of our relationship with God. Regularity in such practices of the virtue of religion is a key to continued spiritual growth.

The Christian virtues are rooted in prayer. Prayer is important at any age. My parents still pray a decade of the rosary every night. At times, we need more silent time to pray. This can be hard to achieve if we have a noisy, bustling daily life. We are used to noise. Noise surrounds us on the road, at work and in stores. We create noise ourselves as well. As soon as we come into a room we need to turn on the radio, the television, the CD player or the computer. Or we need to talk on the telephone. At times, we seem to flee silence. Yet we need some silence in our lives to listen to God—to listen for the inspirations of the Holy Spirit. Even if we find time and a quiet place, we can find silence difficult. It can be difficult to sit still for even five minutes to listen to God. I can testify personally to this difficulty! There always seems to be outside interruptions—a knock on the door, a phone call. And our interior noise—our "to do" lists, our worries—can interrupt us as well. Yet if we persist,

God does speak to us. God gives us surprising insights into our daily situations. Silent prayer—even if only for a few minutes—enhances the practice of humor, humility and patience.

The grace of the Holy Spirit

God the Father speaks to us in prayer through the Holy Spirit, the Third Person of the Trinity. The Holy Spirit, referred to as the "Holy Ghost" when I was a boy, continues to be active in the church, bringing grace into our hearts.

The Spirit is at the heart of the riches of the Catholic Tradition. Our hope rests in the conviction that the Holy Spirit has been leading us down through the centuries and will continue to be our community's guide. Saints such as Augustine and Jane de Chantal, and contemporary martyrs, are led by the Spirit. The gifts of the Spirit, distributed widely in the community, work together for the common good.

Jesus promised to send us his Spirit. The Spirit helps us to understand more fully the truth of Christ's message. The Holy Spirit is the spirit of truth. We are to grasp the truth of Christ more fully and to let it transform our lives. The Spirit transforms our humanness into Christ. The Spirit of Christ touches us in ways too numerous to count. In moments of personal prayer, we can at times feel the healing and consoling power of Christ's presence. When we place our cares and concerns, our worries and anxieties, before God, they frequently diminish. Christ, who sends us his Spirit, really does care about us and helps us with the trials of life.

The Spirit guides the church in a special way through the sacraments. Grace, the divine life, the effect of the Spirit, comes to us through them. For instance, in the sacrament of penance or reconciliation, our deepest hurts and alienations can be healed. Our tragic choices and their consequences can yield to the infinite power of God's love. If we can bring ourselves to acknowledge our faults, which is no easy task, we can experience the warmth of God's healing love. Through the forgiveness of sins, the Spirit can touch us and give us peace.

The work of the Spirit is also in healing and building a community. The tongues of flame, which energized the early apostles, made them a community of faith. Subsequently, the gifts of the Spirit characterized their lives. The Spirit transformed their relationships; they shared all in common. They burned to share their gifts with others.

Living in the Spirit transforms *our* relationships as well. They focus more outward. We become more concerned with the well-being of others than with our own. Our relationships become more characterized by concern for the spiritual growth and well-being of our friends than with our own control and comfort.

Living in the Spirit, we become a healing, vital presence for others. Ultimately, we live in faith, hope and love, joyfully sharing the Spirit of Jesus.

Chapter Two

The Theological Virtues
of Faith, Hope and Love

F aith, hope and love—these most characteristic Christian virtues are the
work of the Holy Spirit in our hearts.
St. Paul reminds us in his letters that these virtues
are intrinsic to the Christian life (for example, in
1 Cor 13:13). But how do we possess them in
practice? What is our experience of these virtues
that are so central to the Christian life? How
might we grow in these virtues?

Our experience of faith

How do we use our time, our energy, and our
money? The answer to this brief question helps us to reveal

our real priorities. The answer shows where we really put our faith.

A common tendency in our culture is to *put faith in having things.* Money can buy the latest consumer goods. Money can make us happy. This is the message of modern advertising. The things money can buy—a Mercedes, a laptop, a pair of the right shoes—can really satisfy us.

Perhaps we put our energy into *achieving success.* Having the right job and gaining recognition from the right people makes us feel good. They fill our need for affirmation and self-worth.

We may use a great deal of our time *to get things under control.* We need to make our own decisions. We do it our way. We actualize ourselves. We may feel uncomfortable if we are not able to plan our future and thus achieve security. Every moment of life must bend to our choices. At the extreme, as with the advocates of assisted suicide, even death itself must be under our control!

A practical faith that gives the priority to possessions, success or control is far removed from the religious faith many of us learned as children. Contemporary faith seems to put material things or our egos in place of God. As a boy, one thing I learned was that faith had to do with knowledge. Catholics believed what God revealed to us as conveyed by the church. We memorized the content of the Baltimore Catechism. Faith involved believing a set of propositions. Faith called for an intellectual assent to the truths of faith.

When I was a young man, this limited understanding of faith set me up for a great challenge. Perhaps I should put my faith in science? Maybe scientific theories could explain life better than these religious propositions? Science was very rational and had "evidence" drawn from experiments. Maybe the theory of evolution was the key to life's meaning? Luckily, I didn't experience this crisis for very long. I found that science is valuable but fails to provide the full meaning of life. Science has its limitations. As with other faith substitutes, it offers only a partial solution to the mystery of life.

Today the emphasis seems to have shifted away from grasping the truths of faith. Now we seek a faith that responds to our personal interests and concerns. Kids say "I'm bored with church." I believe that more than a few adults say the same. Sunday Mass with its ritual and its slower pace does nothing for them. If they come to church at all, they are passive and self-absorbed spectators to the mystery of faith.

The missing element in a bored or skeptical faith is an encounter with Jesus. This goes well beyond the propositions of faith to an assent of soul. When we meet Jesus, our lives change most profoundly. He satisfies our personal interests while drawing us out of ourselves. We may meet Jesus in the Scripture, in the saints of the Catholic tradition or in the charity of our neighbor. The experience may come suddenly with an emotional high, or as gradually as getting to know a friend.

After we meet Jesus, life is different. Our boredom begins to dissipate. Our Sunday Eucharist becomes a time to listen and learn from him. The prayers, the Scriptures and the petitions speak more to our heart. At communion, we can sense his presence. We become Christians in a much deeper way. Like all friendship, our friendship with Christ grows if we speak with him. Our conversation with him is in prayer. Here we both listen and respond. Here the life of faith begins to grow. Here our knowledge of the faith takes on a deeper meaning.

This spiritual life transforms the way we see the world. We begin to develop more balance. Both material possessions and our controlling egos are put in proper perspective. Things are to be used for the good of others; personal gifts are to build a community of love. Eventually this faith begins to penetrate all the aspects of our lives. My work as an administrator is no longer just a series of tasks to be done or meetings to endure. These can provide me with opportunities to show Christ's love to others and to give others the respect they deserve. The more I pray about the events of the day, the more I let go of my need to control them. The more I am a man of faith, the happier I am.

In friendship with Jesus our lives become much more integrated. Faith in him makes us whole. The virtue of faith answers our search for life's meaning. It is strength from God transforming our deepest human needs. Faith in Jesus and commitment to his teachings provides a positive framework for living in our world. Our faith in him redirects our lives and makes for an increasing hope.

The journey of hope

Some people seem naturally hopeful. To them, a glass of water is always half full, their drive from the tee will land a few inches from the cup and the possibilities for the future are endless. For others, the glass is half empty, the drive will land in the sand trap and the future is fraught with obstacles. "Hope springs eternal" is a wise popular saying. People want to be hopeful in spite of their predisposition to pessimism. They keep playing golf despite the sand traps, and look for longer drives in days ahead. For Christians, hope is both a real disposition toward daily life and a virtue. The virtue of hope comes into our hearts with the arrival of the Holy Spirit. The three theological virtues—faith, hope and love—come with the third person of the Trinity. The Spirit's divine grace gives us hope. In baptism, as we receive the Holy Spirit, we begin the journey of hope.

This Christian hope is a gift. It comes from God. We nourish it in personal and communal prayer. Our deepest potential for hope is only gradually developed as we grow spiritually in our relationships with God and others. Over time, even personal disposition can yield to the fire of the Spirit's hope in our hearts. The Catechism of the Catholic Church (#1517) speaks of hope as the "virtue by which we desire the kingdom of heaven and eternal life." Hope orients us to the future. Our heavenly home beckons to us. But in many ways that future is now. We already share, modestly to be sure, in the life of the Spirit, the life of eternity. This grace orients us to our ultimate destiny and empowers us to act right now. Hope is a spiritual energy. It propels us into the future.

Hope pulls us out of ourselves. It urges us to positive acts of goodness toward our neighbor. A cheery good morning, an expression of concern for the sick, or our attentive listening to a colleague can express our hope. A host of small actions can show a hopeful attitude. Hope brings us into daily solidarity with others. Hope can persist despite our disabilities. Each of us is weak. We are deficient in many ways. We have our "blue Mondays" or our "blue anydays." Our physical burdens discourage us. We fear being dependent.

Sometimes our hope disappears. Buffeted by the crises and disappointments of life, despairing of achieving our most cherished dreams and aspirations, depressed by death and destruction, we walk through dark corridors with no hope. We who used to tread so vibrantly now proceed listlessly. As we walk, we gaze outward with a forlorn and empty look. Our eyes focus without comprehension. We can look neither up toward the heavens nor down to the earth. We are drawn deep within. We focus on our darkness and our pain. Certain images repeat themselves again and again. Our minds rerun the same thoughts over and over as we seek to make sense of the difficult, the painful, the absurd. Obscure and dark emotions run their wild way unrestrained.

How might hope be restored? Periods of darkness often have to run their course. There is no shortcut, for example, in the process of grief that brings gradual healing after the death of a loved one or after a major trauma in life. Healing takes time. Its cycle extends for months and years. The process often lasts longer than we would prefer. During this time the warmth of caring family members and friends is all-important. They help us by listening to us with head and heart. They understand our distress. They sense some of what is going on inside us. They affirm that we are still lovable despite our hurts, our failures and our shattered ideals. Their presence brings light into our darkness. If only for a brief moment, they break the dark inner cycle of reflection

How might hope be restored? As a young man, St. Francis de Sales (d. 1622) had a profound crisis of hope. This crisis persisted for weeks. He thought he would be damned for eternity. He found hope again in prayer. At a critical moment, praying in Paris before a statue of Our Lady known as the Black Madonna, he gave himself completely to God. The crisis resolved. Later, he became known as one of the most optimistic of saints.

Prayer is a key to hope. In prayer, we enter into a special relationship with God, often through the good example and intercession of Mary and the saints. In prayer, we are present to God. This may mean our wordless presence in a chapel or church. We may not have the spiritual energy to act, to speak or to think at all. Yet our being present to God is enough. God knows our hearts.

Our unique friendship with God sustains us in hope. The inner obstacles to hope—our disquieting thoughts and feelings—quite often surface in our time of prayer and can be offered to Christ for healing. Gradually we come to realize that disappointment and death may bring us to healing and strength. Here the paradox of the cross becomes part of our real knowledge. As St. Paul said, it is when we are weak that we are strong. We live once again in hope for heaven and for God's grace today. We know that progress is always possible. But we have changed. Our restored hope is different. It is deeper. We now have a more realistic view of our hope for earth and for eternity. Not without detours, discouragement and disasters does hope on earth prepare us for heaven.

God's grace can transform even a reluctant heart. Our personal limitations can make our solidarity with those in need quite real. An alcoholic now in recovery, for example, is often the most powerful witness to hope for the person still struggling with alcoholism. Our hope despite our weaknesses may enable others to hope as well. It is precisely in our weakness that we are best able to put our talents at God's service. We realize that hope ultimately is in God.

Such a hopeful person embraces substantive projects for the good of others. He or she seeks to change the neighborhood, the city, civil society and even the whole country. And doesn't take no for an answer! Hopeful people see that the reign of God begins now and requires intensive effort. While this world will never be heaven, it can be better with God's help. Hopeful people are people of light, not of darkness. Their focus on the light of eternity enables them to enlighten the earth.

Love

Our reflections on faith and hope lead us to the central virtue of all—Christian love. Without love, there are no other Christian virtues. Without love there is no Christianity! Jesus lived a life of love. Jesus showed us how to love. Love is central to Jesus' teaching. Jesus linked love of God and love of our neighbor.

I'll always remember my first visit years ago to our local Catholic infants' home, St. Ann's. The little children

there—only a few years old—came up and grabbed all the visitors around the legs! We were startled and immobilized for a moment. The children were looking for a human touch. They had been deprived of love at home and were looking for signs of love from the staff and even from visitors. Our natural desire for love is hard to suppress. These children showed it spontaneously.

Love is natural. It often expresses itself in touch. Babies need to be held. Children need to be hugged. In fact, no matter what our age, we all need a hug once in a while—a daily hug or two is preferable. We never cease needing love. Most of us are appreciative of a little loving attention. This is very evident when we are incapacitated or isolated—in the hospital or far away on a business trip or in a nursing home. A visit, a telephone call, a note or an e-mail all express in a tangible way that loving friendship which makes us and keeps us human. In all the stages of the life cycle, we need love.

We not only need love from others but we can give it. Love is the most precious thing we have to give. My parents, now grandparents for many years, give love to my nieces and nephews on a regular basis through things such as gifts, overnight visits, birthday meals and attendance at school events. This past Christmas, two of my young nieces reciprocated by taking their grandparents out to lunch! I'm sure it was a wonderful meal. In such everyday acts, love is sustained and developed. I am especially happy that this loving spirit is so evident in the next generation in my own family.

Love can grow throughout life. My own observation and that of many other people is that couples' love grows deeper when they have children. Having and caring for a child is an exhausting experience, especially right after birth! Yet it changes the focus of life as well. Loving parents naturally focus on their new child and lessen their focus on themselves. Their perception of the world changes as well. Relatives, friends, babysitters, neighborhoods and schools become much more important. Love widens the circle of concern. After childbirth, couples' perception of faith and the church community often changes as well. Love makes us want to share the most important things in life with our children.

A few years ago, within a ten-day period I performed three baptisms. These were baptisms for the children of couples whose wedding Masses I had celebrated in previous years. Each brought together a different set of relatives and friends. Each was a festive and loving event—recorded for posterity with videos and pictures. Each brought together several generations to share love with each other as God shared love with them. Each baptism was a transformative moment. The Holy Spirit transformed each child interiorly—bringing the Christian virtues of faith, hope and love. Each child is now a Christian. The Spirit of love, the Holy Spirit, has begun the inner transformation that will continue throughout a lifetime.

The Holy Spirit transforms the family and friends gathered as well. The parents and godparents assume a special spiritual role by agreeing to raise the child to be a loving Christian. The friends and family affirm their faith and their own dedication to Christian love. In this sacrament, the spiritual or supernatural dimension of love comes to the fore. We are made in God's image; thus we are made to love. The grace of the Holy Spirit enables us to love most fully.

Love is a feeling. Joy, humor and warm family feeling filled these celebrations. In one instance, my tiny cousin decided to move her head at the very moment of baptism. Water went everywhere. The family was concerned, then amused. She cried her disapproval!

Love is a commitment. We give our children and ourselves to God. God gives himself to us in the inner life of the Holy Spirit. The Holy Spirit touches the deepest part of our soul

Love grows. As we go through adulthood, we can become more loving. The grace of the Spirit can redirect our lives. The Spirit helps us to let go of the unnecessary, such as excessive concern for material goods, to grasp and to prioritize the essential, such as time for family outings and events.

Love is a virtue. Like all virtues, it integrates and transforms our thinking, our knowing and our feeling.

Love is the central virtue. Our love forms our lives. Our love touches others. Our love reflects God's love. Our love lasts eternally.

Chapter Three

Moral Virtues for Every Day

*D*aily life invites and sometimes forces us to practice a variety of virtues. These virtues, varied manifestations of Christian love, are often not very noticeable. They are not the stuff of news headlines. But they form the character of our daily lives. We will sample a few such virtues in this chapter. I will begin with the virtue of humor, a virtue already mentioned in chapter one. Humor helps us keep our priorities in order.*

Humor

       I can't remember jokes. Try as I might, remembering one joke at a time is my limit. I enjoy listening to others telling jokes. A few years ago a priest colleague came into my office and told me twenty minutes straight of jokes—many from memory—that he was using for a "roast" of a mutual friend. I thoroughly enjoyed it, but I couldn't tell you one joke he said after he walked out the door.

I'm glad that humor is more than joking. Humor can be glaringly obvious or a subtle play on words. Humor can be a joke with a punch line or an ironic twist of a phrase. Humor can bring a smile or a belly laugh. Humor has many sides, many dimensions. Humor is a way of looking at life, a way of laughing at the incongruities. Humor provides us with perspective on the ups and downs of life. Humor often involves laughing at ourselves. Our mistakes and idiosyncrasies are the stuff of an inward smile, if not an outright laugh. It's good not to take ourselves too seriously. We are not so perfect.

In the parish where I celebrate the Eucharist each Sunday, there are a host of characters. One man absentmindedly stands up for the Gospel and remains standing for the homily. He is not protesting anything! After a few minutes of the preaching, he either sits down or walks to the back of church—whichever suits him. People are quite tolerant of his unusual behavior. He is a parish "character." Or at least he is an obvious one. We are all parish characters in our own way. Some of us may just be a little better at keeping our idiosyncrasies hidden. But we certainly do bring them with us and let them show inadvertently some Sundays, perhaps at the coffee hour after Mass.

Sometimes I think that God must be amused at all that he sees going on each Sunday—the miscues, the little distractions, the singing off-key and the children who really come for the donuts after Mass. God certainly does seem to have a sense of humor. I sometimes wonder about divine providence. Over thirty years ago I chose religious life in the Oblates of St. Francis de Sales and the vow of poverty. Yet for almost two decades I have held positions that require either the raising of money or the management of it or both. I wonder if God laughs at the incongruity of it. I thought I was minimizing material concerns with the vow, only to embrace them again in new ways.

Certainly we can learn to accept divine providence with humor. Humor is a certain type of virtue. We can learn about humor and develop a sense of humor. Good humor can become a trait of our character. We can become a joy to be around. I think of good humor as being a virtue that is a dimension of joy. The joyful person can see the humorous side of life.

Sometimes we can lose our joy and the humor that is a part of it. Our humor can veer into the areas of put-down or prejudice. Not-so-good humor is destructive. Eventually such sinful "humor" destroys our inner joy. True joy builds up others. *Good* humor is not destructive.

The stresses of life can also cause us to lose our joy. When life's tragedies hit us hard we can be really humorless for months or even years while coping with our loss. But as the dark clouds lift, we can begin to see the light. Humor is a barometer of our inner health. One sign of our recovery is the return of our good sense of humor and inner joy.

A religious community can help with this healing process. The lighthearted banter and the kidding about human faults characteristic of such communities can be supportive of our human endeavors. Laughter can bring people together. It can be part of the glue of human communities. Ideally a joy pervades our Christian communities when they are at their best.

Civility

A second binding virtue for Christian communities and for civil society is civility. Civility is a key dimension of personal Christian character and of Christian communities. It is a virtue greatly needed in society today.

In following political campaigns or political scandals, in watching television and listening to the radio, we can easily learn the language of incivility. Hyperbole easily slides into public discussion. An opponent is a "liar," a "Nazi," an "extremist" or "narrow-minded." Civility is absent in such harmful affronts to a person's integrity or character.

We treat others civilly because we respect them. Each person is made in God's image. God specially calls each person. Each person has wisdom to share. How do we show such respect? Certainly we show respect for others by avoiding demeaning words and conversations. Civility forbids "trash talking," whether in politics, on the fields of sports or at the mall. We show respect by building others up rather than tearing them down. Taking others' ideas and opinions seriously denotes such respect. Civility calls us to respect others' human dignity, even when we disagree with them.

In civility we listen carefully to others to grasp their reasoning and their understanding—to see "where they are coming from." In civility we presume the best motivation in others. We seek the kernel of truth in what they are saying. They are still worthy of respect and love, even if we think they are mistaken! Thus civility avoids hyperbole and sticks to the facts in a discussion. Of course we are all used to the hyperbole in televised speech. I have to smile when a passing sporting event, such as a Super Bowl or a World Series, is described by the media as "historic." Such is not the stuff of history, but of recreation. We are all accustomed to such exaggerations from advertising. A product is described as "the best in the world." We learned long ago to ignore this kind of hype.

Such exaggerations can work against civility. Our media interviews often emphasize the extremes rather than balance and moderation. The most radical and inflammatory individuals present points of view—even if they only represent a handful of people. Such conflict is thought to sell newspapers, magazines and TV shows.

Civility urges a change in such public discourse. Some workplaces too seem devoid of a basic concern for others. Only the "bottom line" or personal success seems to matter in them. In this type of poisonous atmosphere, individuals are devalued and dismissed. Downsizing occurs no matter what the human cost. Personal success must be attained no matter what.

If, as some say, truth is relative, if it can never be attained, then there may be wisdom in being the loudest, the most aggressive or the most hyperbolic. We may then need to be forceful to get our own way. If everything is relative, verbal—and even physical—force counts. Civility, on the contrary, involves respect for others and for the truth.

Even small actions, such as helping an elderly or disabled person, build a civil community.

In our public discourse and discussion, we are engaged in a common search for the truth. Such engagement will not proceed without a touch of humility on the part of all those involved. Recognizing that I might not have the whole truth or that I may be acting in a very self-centered way requires some personal insight and introspection.

Our personalities affect our civility. In fact all virtues are refracted through our unique individuality. Thus we might discover that our absolute convictions reflect the dogmatism we always exhibit. Or, in contrast, these convictions might reflect our need for security in an unstable and changing world. Or they may be the result of a spiritual pilgrimage which has successfully grasped some hard truths.

Civility is a moral imperative if we are to have a democratic and humane society. It rests on the proposition that there is truth to be found. We find this truth in collaboration with others.

If civility is necessary in civil society, it is even more necessary in the church. At a conference one spring, I met a man who recently turned to ministry in a parish after years in the business world. I asked him what he found to be the biggest difference between the two worlds. His answer was that people in the church were much more committed to their work. They had a deeper emotional investment. His answer points positively to the depth of commitment of people to the faith. But it also alerts us to our own need for civility within the Christian community. Since we are so deeply committed emotionally, we can have

a tendency to dismiss the views of others who disagree with us. We can personally excommunicate them!

Long ago St. Paul experienced similar difficulties with the Corinthians. He urged the wisdom of focusing on Christ. Jesus died and rose for the salvation of all. Civility most certainly is a virtue for church and society. Its respect for human dignity is rooted in our deepest understanding of salvation in Jesus Christ.

Solidarity

Solidarity is a natural concomitant to civility. The word solidarity always reminds me of the Polish trade union, Lech Walesa, and the fall of communism. I first thought: How clever of Pope John Paul II to make his favorite trade union into a virtue [in his 1987 encyclical *Sollicitudo Rei Socialis*]! Only later, in reading the catechism, did I find the Pope Pius XII mention of solidarity in 1939.

The word solidarity has a European ring to it. Americans might rather speak of friendship, community and the works of charity. Yet, solidarity with others in the communion of saints is a central dimension of our faith, which we mention in praying the creed each Sunday. It means that we are to share our spiritual and material goods with one another. We are to work together for the common good.

Solidarity implies mutuality. We are a community of believers. However, we differ in age, race, education, and upbringing and in so many other ways. We have a lot to learn from one another. We must learn to listen with head and heart. In solidarity, we learn that even our poorest and most eccentric community members have gifts to offer and important things to say. This is not to imply that all are equally gifted or insightful. Rather, wise judgment is open to the multiple ways God speaks to us through others.

Solidarity seeks the common good. One striking thing about the mass suicide of the cultists near San Diego a few years ago was their self-concern. They limited themselves to seeking their own transcendence and their destiny in outer space. They seemed to give little thought to others. Their isolated communal search for life's meaning led to their demise.

The truth is that our deepest longings are fulfilled not in fleeing into outer space, but in engaging our neighbor. We are made to be with and for others. We grow best when we share our spiritual and material goods out of deep respect for one another.

Solidarity implies commitment. We commit ourselves to respect those who are different from ourselves. Every year on January 22 I attend the March for Life here in Washington. The crowd is diverse and interesting. It is a friendly coalition of varied groups. There is always someone handing out literature or wishing to engage in conversation. We are one in our commitment to the unborn. While diverse in religious background, we respect one another while pursuing our common purpose.

Such solidarity creates power. Together we are strong. Together we can work for the common good in service to the unborn, the elderly or the disadvantaged. Together we can pursue a just social order.

The deepest dimension of living comes in serving others. We experience transcendence as we serve others.

Such service calls for the deepest, and often unrealized, spiritual resources within our hearts and souls.

Our solidarity is in Christ. Jesus blesses our community with many gifts and talents. When we are at our best—not that we always are—we share these for the good of all. Christ blesses us with the talents of good leaders. Our contemporary saints—each of us probably knows at least one holy person—teach us what solidarity in Christ really means in practice.

Service to others is characteristic of such leadership in Christ. In solidarity, the leader humbly washes the feet of others as Jesus did at the Last Supper.[2]

Many years ago, St. Augustine noted that "Our hearts are restless 'til they rest in thee." Our solidarity with others leads us to eternal life. Our ultimate solidarity will be with the saints in heaven. Now we experience that imperfect yet genuine solidarity which works for a just and flourishing community on earth. Here we respect human dignity. Here we value each person's gifts.

The word solidarity still reminds me of a labor union. But this virtue also reminds me that I am most myself when I am in union with others. When I am seeking to understand and learn from others, I am being my best self.

Understanding

Who is the best teacher you ever had? I'm sure that you can recall one or perhaps several teachers rather quickly. I can name a few of mine that were in the very first rank. They were skilled in maintaining interest and conveying information. They increased my understanding of their subject. They are with me still in my memory of their material and of their enthusiasm for teaching.

Understanding, of course, is not just for the classroom. I have had—and I'm sure you have too—many teachers who were not in school. I've learned the most from those who have a deep understanding of people. They have a "knowledge of the heart" that rivals formal learning. One good friend says he learns the most by continually studying other people. This study involves both seeing and listening. We see others—how they act, the example they give—and we learn from them. We listen to others and drink in their wisdom.

Such listening can be difficult, however. We have many external and internal barriers to understanding. There is so much *noise* around us that we learn not to listen. We only half pay attention in our conversations at home or at work. Another barrier is *the numerous internal "hurts" or " bad memories" we have.* These are the scars of living. They—and the emotions attached to them—can prevent us from really grasping what another is saying by speaking in the classroom, or by example or in conversation. Understanding involves getting past these obstacles. With God's grace, we can be healed. And we can learn to listen with head and heart.

Understanding even embraces listening to those who disagree with us. They may be speaking God's word in ways that are unfamiliar or challenging to our preconceptions. Thus understanding calls for a fair amount of humility. We need to acknowledge our lack of understanding. We have to admit that we don't have all the answers.

We have a lot to learn—and our teachers may be the most unlikely people.

Understanding involves the search for the fullness of truth about our own humanity. Years ago I noted in the history exhibit at the Dachau concentration camp the philosophical errors which nourished Nazi oppression. Their misconceptions of our human nature justified wars, concentration camps and "final solutions." Coming to an understanding of the truth of the human person is absolutely essential for our own good and for the good of society. This search for the fullness of truth never ends.

Our capacity to know things and people grows over time. Parents look for the developmental patterns in their young children. They seek to know what their children are capable of understanding about God and the world so as to instruct them most effectively. Even as adults we can continually grow in understanding. We only see part of the picture. We need the help of others. Our own limited or biased understandings can be corrected and developed.

We can often understand things and people better if we talk our perceptions through with a friend. Just talking things through—attempting to put our ideas into words—can increase our understanding. Friends also offer us insights that expand our own.

As adults we are familiar with many ways of knowing. We can know things through scientific understanding. While theirs is not the only way of knowing, sciences such as physics, chemistry and biology do offer us powerful tools for understanding the physical world.

We can know through artistic creativity. An artist may have a more intuitive or creative way of looking at the world. A friend of mine who is a sculptor recently gave me a small marble statue of my patron, St. John the Evangelist. I will spend years, I'm sure, trying to gain insight into this abstract, meditative, seated figure. All my sculptor friend would say about it was that it looks different from different angles!

We can know through divine revelation. God shares his life with us. There is both understanding and mystery in this revelation. We can know the truths of faith but not completely. They are mysteries of faith, which we can always understand better.

Like Mary we need to treasure all these things in our hearts. We need time to ponder in depth—and slowly—the mystery of God's work in salvation history. We reflect on God's working in our own lives. We ponder the magnificence of human artistic creations as they speak to us of human creativity and divine goodness. We marvel at the wonders of the physical universe that is made known to us in science.

Ultimately, we seek understanding of God's work in our hearts. The great saints and mystics tell us that God comes to us, embraces us, in the deepest forms of prayer. Here our understanding gives way to the experience of the divine.

Understanding is a virtue for earth and for heaven. For in seeing God face-to-face we will come to a fullness of loving understanding that grows for eternity.

Chapter Four

Cultivating Virtues Daily

*T*he virtues for daily living that we have been discussing become ingrained as a result of practice. *We are creatures of habit. To progress in living the life of virtue, we need to embrace practices—specific and regular ways of acting in collaboration with the grace of the Holy Spirit—that will become habitual. These freely chosen ways of acting form our lives for holiness.*

The Importance of Freedom

Recently I taught a class on freedom to a group of teenagers. I told them that they must freely choose to be women or men of faith. No one—parents, priests, teachers or friends—can choose for them. No one can make them be a Catholic Christian. Their attentiveness to this early-morning message was palpable. The usual lassitude gave way to attention. Talk of freedom enlivened them.

Freedom is very important to most Americans—teenagers included. We live in "the land of the free." Our Constitution and the Bill of Rights guarantee our freedom. We like being free. Americans of any age resonate to freedom. We want to be free to believe what we choose. We want to make up our own minds. And we want to speak our minds.

Our concern to speak whatever is on our minds can be a source of either admiration or amazement to others. This past fall I participated in a group discussion with a woman from Africa. She had just come to the United States to study. She marveled at our freedom of expression. In fact, she mentioned that if people in her country criticized the government—a dictatorship—as she heard Americans doing, they and their families would disappear! Another partici-pant—also from Africa—continued the discussion by com-menting on the lack of restraint American freedom showed. Almost any view—no matter how extreme or corrupting—seemed acceptable. He was amazed at our use of freedom. He questioned the common American view that freedom is "to do as I please as long as I don't hurt anyone." He linked freedom and moral responsibility.

These views of people from other cultures give us pause to examine our emphasis, or overemphasis, on free-dom. The Christian view of human freedom challenges our extremes. Christians believe that freedom is good.

Made in God's image, we are made to be free. But freedom is only one part of the total picture. A realistic person needs to examine the whole question.

A brief look at our personal history can convince us of this need. A friend of mine writes of his "broken past," his difficult upbringing, which affects him even now in his retirement. Each of us has some brokenness within us that cries out for healing and redemption. We are all in need of redemption. We are far from self-sufficient. Yet, providentially God has chosen us and begun to heal us of our sin and self-destruction.

We walk around with the scars of living. We have had disappointments, tragedies and betrayals. Others have used their freedom to harm us. And we have used our freedom to harm ourselves! We have not chosen wisely. We have sometimes chosen vice rather than virtue. Some of us struggle with addictions—to drugs or alcohol. A recent national report speaks of the addiction of many—perhaps millions—to gambling. We are not as free as we like to think we are. Many more of us struggle with our pasts in less radical ways. We have graphic memories that haunt us. We have negative habits formed long ago which are hard to break. We have certain negative ways of thinking about people and situations.

We all know a person in the office or neighborhood who always sees the downside of everything. He or she is quick to criticize the boss, a coworker or the person next door. Somehow this person is never responsible; it is always someone else's fault!

One glory of our freedom is that with God's grace, we can regain it. We can leave behind our negative ways of thinking and acting. We can build up those at the office rather than talking them down. We can choose to practice virtue. We can move away from our tragic past. One friend has done this by praying about the situation and then writing about it in a personal journal. The process of putting his tragedy on paper was itself cathartic. Several people I know have talked about their brokenness with a spiritual friend. Many others have given the past over to the healing power of Christ through the sacrament of reconciliation.

The song *Amazing Grace* is both popular and true. It speaks to the problems and possibilities of the human condition. We can freely choose to let our wretchedness be saved by Christ. Thus we can enter into a period of ongoing conversion that will last for a lifetime. Only in heaven will we experience the fullness of human freedom.

Conversion is ongoing

My friend Harry used to love to ride his motorcycle—fast. He rode it to work in downtown Washington almost every day. One afternoon, when he was zipping home in the fast lane in the middle of rush-hour traffic, he experienced a blowout of one of his tires. Somehow he got from the fast lane over to the shoulder of the road without being killed. As Harry will tell you to this day, that incident, that brush with death, caused him to reevaluate his life. He gave up his motorcycle. And he went from being what he calls a good "Sunday Catholic" to being much more. He experienced a deeper conversion and began to make his faith an everyday priority. Such a conversion is a major turnabout, not just a minor revision. A personal conversion makes Christ central every day and causes us to change our priorities. Practically speaking, we schedule our time accordingly. We put our prayer time in the best time of the day. We don't just "wedge it in" after we settle everything else.

Recently, I was one of the presenters at an Engaged Encounter Weekend. One of the key points of this experience of marriage preparation is that the couple must go from being an *I* to being a *We*. They must continue to move from being self-centered to being other-centered. To succeed at this major reorientation, they need to look at the patterns of their lives and begin to change them. They must make "prime time" for each other—not just "any old time." And if they are to succeed, they need to see Christ in their relationship and make time for him as well.

I believe that there are many similarities between our personal need for repentance and conversion and the needs of the church. These similarities leapt out at me as I was reading Pope John Paul II's letter on the third millennium.[3] In his letter the Holy Father reviews many of the good things which have happened in the history of the church—such as the spread of the faith throughout the world and the development of the church's social teaching. Yet he is quite realistic in acknowledging the ongoing need for repentance. We, members of the church, are sinners and need to repent. He says: "Although she is holy because of her incorporation into Christ, the church does not tire of doing penance" (#33).

The pope realistically acknowledges past history. The closing millennium has been one of divisions within Christendom. The ruptures with the Orthodox and with the Protestant churches are two examples that spring immediately to mind. As the Second Vatican Council acknowledged, at times people on both sides were responsible for such ruptures. The Holy Father notes that "Ecclesial Communion has been painfully wounded" (#34).

I have seen these divisions up close in my work as executive director of the Consortium of Catholic and Protestant theological schools in the Washington area. The divisions are real and occasionally painful. Yet our institutions' willingness to work together, to communicate effectively and to renew our ecumenical collaboration—with attention to the guidance of the Holy Spirit—is a hopeful sign of the new millennium.

As with individuals, realistic acknowledgement of the past can set the stage for healing and future growth. The Holy Father notes that our past includes "acquiescence given, especially in certain centuries, to intolerance and even the use of violence, in the service of truth" (#35). While we certainly seek to understand individuals in their own historical context, we must acknowledge the weaknesses and sinfulness of so many of our predecessors in the faith.

Original Sin is with us still. In particular, it seems to me that intolerance of others who differ from us in race, ethnicity or religion is still present with us today. We need ongoing conversion

As the Second Vatican Council said: "The truth cannot impose itself except by virtue of its own truth, as it wins over the mind by both gentleness and power" (*Declaration on Religious Freedom*, #1). Thus there is no room for coercion of persecution. We must rather engage in a common search for truth. We believe that this search will lead us to Christ. We, for our part, need to listen attentively for God.

Listening to God

In the midst of our ordinary lives, God speaks to us. Though surrounded by a seemingly secular world, we can hear God speak in our daily lives. This communication may be wordless. The beauty of the sunset, the wonder of galaxies of the cosmos and the intricacy of DNA speak of the simplicity, the complexity and the mystery of life. The wonders of nature lead us to question their origin and goal—and our own. Like the poet, we ponder God's grandeur.

God often speaks to us through the example of others. Silent example speaks volumes. Recently, a couple I know buried one of their sons. He was disabled—but of course only in some ways. Twenty-two years of quiet devotion and self-sacrificing love speak wordlessly of this couple's priorities and their faith. Some human actions need no commentary. Good example points to the deeper, more important realities that can be ignored in the rush of daily living. It speaks to us of God.

Through the transitions and crises of life, God speaks. The quick pace of ordinary living often distorts the divine message. We can't hear it very clearly. Our ears tune in to other louder messages. But periodically the pain of change, of suffering or of death interrupts our ordinary listening and grabs our attention. It reminds us of ultimate

realities. It reminds us of our mortality. Earthly life ends. We are here only for a time.

In the mysterious depths of our consciousness, when we are quiet and still, God speaks to us about our basic humanity. He shows us life's purpose. He speaks to us about loving.

> Love serves others.
> Love humanizes us.
> Love endures.

Some of my friends seem to me to be "restless for God"—always seeking this deeper love. They are present-day Saint Augustines, always probing for his will. They are not content with themselves or with the present. Their inner spirit seeks something more.

> One seeks a new mission in life.
> Another dwells each morning in silent prayer.
> A third hesitates between teaching and direct service.
> A fourth probes the virtues of parenthood.

How can we take God for granted when he speaks to us so continuously?

Our perceptions depend on our spirit's "framework for living." We can live each day focused on work, success, possessions, sports and entertainment. These are all good in themselves. Yet Christians have a different way of looking at the world. They gradually come to see God at work in the midst of these everyday attributes of life. The grandeur of creation, the love of a family, the example of friends, and the restless search for the deepest love speak of God's mysterious presence in our midst.

People can't easily take God for granted because he reaches out and touches them. Occasionally he speaks directly; often he whispers in the gentle breeze.

As Christians see things, our freedom is for the good, for the true and for the beautiful. It is the freedom to be our best selves. What are we free for? Put succinctly, we are free to be holy. Nothing else really matters. We are free to be holy—to be like Christ. We are free to give everything—tragedies, scars, successes and even our inmost thoughts—to God.

Resources for growing spiritually

We have so many things to be thankful for! Yet, how frequently we focus on what we don't have—or on the things others have! In reality we have great riches. We ought to count our blessings every day. As we grow toward spiritual maturity, we begin to appreciate much more what God has given us. Our attitude begins to shift. We begin to treasure our blessings rather than count our mistakes, our sufferings and our losses.

We are loved infinitely by God. This is our prime resource! He knew us before we were born. We don't earn his love. It just is. All we can do is respond in love. We can let our lives be guided by the Holy Spirit, the spirit of love.

A key resource for growing spiritually is our choice. In gratitude we choose to follow the inner inspirations of the Holy Spirit. We recommit ourselves wholeheartedly to the spiritual journey. This commitment takes time.

We need to set aside time—and prime time at that—to pray. There is no substitute for regularity in prayer. We need to pray every day. Prayer is more like the marathon than the hundred-yard dash. Patience, pace and consistency are important.

As mentioned above, we humans are creatures of habit. I notice this in church on Sunday. People tend to go to the same Mass and sit in the same place in the same pew each week. They even tend to get upset if someone else sits in their spot in their pew! Some people come early, some arrive barely on time and others "slide in" before the Gospel. These are habits built up over the years. We may need to develop new habits of prayer if we are to grow spiritually.

One friend I know gets up half an hour early, while the house is still quiet, to spend time in prayer. Other friends seek out a quiet chapel or a daily Mass for some "quality time" with God.

Our friendship with God, like all our other friendships, needs time for communication and sharing. Our life of prayer, with its listening for God's word and our response, is an ongoing relationship.

My married friends seem to be in constant communication with each other. They frequently are on the phone with each other, or sending e-mails back and forth. Their love expresses itself in communication. So too does our love for God.

In this context of prayerful communication, we take the opportunities for spiritual growth that the day provides. A positive morning greeting or a small act of kindness can brighten up our environment with a little love. These small acts of life are inconspicuous and amazingly fruitful. During the day, instead of rushing from place to place, we might slow down enough to murmur a short prayer for the people we encounter, for our relatives or for the sick. All prayers do not need to be formal or lengthy. Some of the best are short and in our own words.

Other prayerful words come to us from the Bible. The Bible not only is a direct means of communication of God to us, but is also a splendid source of vocabulary for our own prayer. As we study the Scriptures, we learn who God is—especially through his Son Jesus Christ. As we study the Scriptures, we learn as well how the biblical authors spoke to God. And we might find ourselves imperceptibly learning their language.

Our biblically-based spirituality need not be merely personal. In fact, it is better if it is not "Jesus and me." Many Americans belong to small learning or sharing groups. You might consider joining such a group or small community for Scripture study or spiritual sharing. The sharing of spiritual experiences can be quite moving. When we see and learn about the struggles and spiritual maturity of others, we are inspired toward holiness ourselves. Other community members can gently challenge us to be our best selves. They can provide both example and words of encouragement. When we encounter the inevitable disappointments and sufferings in life, spiritual friends in a community are invaluable. They are the prime resource God provides for spiritual growth and constancy as we struggle. Recently I noticed that a man at church, whose wife had died a few months previously, seemed to be enjoying socializing with his friends after Mass in the parish hall. In a real way, they were helping him to bear the new burden of life alone.

Communities provide challenge and support. Communities also provide wisdom.

Our Catholic tradition offers a host of resources for coming to spiritual maturity. One important resource is the writings of the saints. As we mature spiritually, we begin to wonder where we are going. Or we may fear that we are going in the wrong direction! Lucky for us, the saints have outlined the stages of spiritual progress. The spiritual life seems to move from the early period of conversion, through a stage of letting go of obstacles to growth, to higher degrees of loving God and neighbor. The contours of the ground are similar for all of us, though the individual paths God leads us along vary infinitely.

The guidance of the saints, the support of a community and the inspired Scriptures are rich resources which aid our growth in friendship with God.

Concluding Reflections

I hope these brief meditations have been of some help to you toward living the virtues each day. Knowledge about the virtues is helpful. Living the virtues is most significant. We often have trouble seeing or believing how the ordinary things—going for a walk with a friend, or driving the children to the game—can be so important for our spiritual progress. Yet these daily events are what we most frequently can give to God in love.

Notes

1. I have developed my reflections more in detail in my *Friendship: The Key to Spiritual Growth* (Mahwah, N.J.: Paulist, 1997) and *Walking in Virtue: Moral Decisions and Spiritual Growth in Daily Life* (Mahwah, N.J.: Paulist, 1998).

2. For more on the virtue of humility, see my *Walking in Virtue*, pp. 87–89.

3. John Paul II, "As the Third Millennium Draws Near," *Origins* 24/24 (November 24, 1994): 401–416.

For Further Reading

The considerations in this book are only a few of the many things which can be said about the life of virtue. For further reading on the spiritual life, you might want to consult Dolores R. Leckey, *Seven Essentials for the Spiritual Journey* (New York: Crossroad, 1999) or Eugene F. Hemrick, *The Promise of Virtue* (Notre Dame: Ave Maria Press, 1999). I believe that continued study helps us in the gradual transformation that is the life of virtue. For a good academic treatment of virtue ethics, see Joseph J. Kotva, Jr., *The Christian Case for Virtue Ethics* (Washington, D.C.: Georgetown University Press, 1996).